The Son Did Rise

(Book of Spiritual Poems)

The Son Did Rise

(Book of Spiritual Poems)

By

Hermeione Flowers

m
p

Old Mountain Press

Published by:
Flowers Publishing
210 Dunbar St.
Allendale, SC 29810

www.oldmp.com/sondidrise.htm

In conjunction with:
Old Mountain Press, Inc.
2542 S. Edgewater Dr.
Fayetteville, NC 28303
www.oldmountainpress.com

Old Mountain Press

Copyright © 2003 Hermeione Flowers
Interior text design by Tom Davis
ISBN: 978-0-9765407-0-0
Library of Congress Control Number: 2005900645

The Son Did Rise (Book of Spiritual Poems).

First Edition
Printed and bound in the United States of America by Morris
Publishing • www.rnorrispublishing.com • 800-650-7888
3 4 5 6 7 8 9 10
Cover Photography Copyright © 1997 by Morris Press

Foreword

*T*o all who love and seek The Lord, Jesus Christ: these words are the Words Of Life that have been preached down in my heart by The Men of God. Once you hear The Gospel of The Kingdom preached, you'll never be the same again! The miracle of being born again is real. Troubles become a stepping-stone, sorrows become joy, hard times become good times and our ways become foolish. The Good News of Jesus Christ is available in this last and evil day! The only safe place is in Jesus Christ! Jesus Christ-The Way, The Truth and The Life! These poems are based on the Doctrine of Jesus Christ.

Contents

Foreword v

Jesus Is Lord 1

The Son Did Rise 2

The Men of God... 3

The Government of Jesus Christ............................... 4

I've Been Saved 5

Cast The First Stone.. 6

Forgive Me Lord 7

Young People Stand... 8

The Blood... 10

The Gospel of The Kingdom Is Being Preached 11

Lord I Thank You 13

Give God The Glory 15

Be Encouraged 16

My Testimony.. 17

A Gangster's Cry 19

Forever 22

God Is... 23

Friend In Jesus 24

Grace Waited 25

Stop It Mr. Bully 26

The Doctor Is In The City 27

The Hidden Man of the Heart 29

Today At Work 30

Out Came The Son.................................32

High Tower 33

Spiritual Picnic.....................................35

When I Am Gone 37

A Wandering Spirit...............................38

Your Presence Lord 40

There Are No Bastard Children 41

Bullies Hate Bullying............................42

Unloved Touch.......................................43

Teach Me Jesus......................................44

Standing At The Crossroad 45

Surrender..46

Remember Me Lord................................47

Soul Food...48

My Soul Is Free......................................49

Inside of A Harasser..............................50

Jesus Is Worthy......................................52

Hold Up Your Light...............................53

If The Son Didn't Shine.........................54

Forgive, Forget......................................55

All About Jesus......................................56

Bright Light...58

A Sinner's Friend 59

Saved By Grace......................................60

Stop Looking and See 61

Magnify Jesus Christ..............................62

A Mother's Love....................................63

A Bully Needs..64

False Accusers 66

I'm Rich 67

Keep Me Lord...68

Jesus Is Mine..69

Pray For Your Enemies..70

Female Harassment..71

Words With Meaning..72

We're Free 73

The Rock...74

Spirit of Harassment 75

Good, Bad, No Credit 77

Repent 78

Female Bully...79

Royal Priesthood...80

Seek The Lord...81

Lover of Lovers...82

Itching Ears 83

Love 84

In The Evening..85

Jesus Is Lord

Jesus is Lord
Respond to Him as such
Jesus is Lord
Without help or a crutch

Jesus is Lord
The Most Honorable Judge
Jesus is Lord
In His ways–indulge

Jesus is Lord
Above, on and below earth
Jesus is Lord
Waiting for you to give His Spirit birth

The Son Did Rise

The Son did rise
Yes, I believe
Early one morning
The most beautiful day
The Son did rise

Things were dark
I needed to see
I needed to live
I needed so badly
For the Son to rise

The Son did rise
Rose in my heart
When it is dark
I can still see
All because
The Son did rise

The Men of God

The Men of God are preaching Jesus
Because they are concerned
Jesus has annointed them
The Body, they can discern

How else will God talk to us
Except through a man
Dismiss the flesh that you see
See inside if you can

(Hebrews 13: 17) "Obey them that have the rule over you"
Through Paul, God has said
Our leaders watch for our souls
How else will we be made?

If we cannot follow
If we cannot obey
We've established our own righteousness
We've established our own way

He said our little righteousness
Is as filthy rags
Stinking in His nostrils
It causes us to brag

Hear the Men of God
Surely, they know the way
Follow them into the kingdom
Hear these men today!

The Government of Jesus Christ

The Government of Jesus Christ
Shall stand forever more
When everything else has failed
Jesus will still be the door

If you want a safe place
Hide in Jesus Christ
For you'll lose nothing
You'll gain all–Eternal life

Put your confidence in His plan
Designed to save sinners
Invest your life in Him
You'll be a blessed winner

For a Conquering King
Is soon to return
All disobedient souls,
Satan and his angels will burn

The Government of Jesus Christ
Shall always stand
It will be the sole survivor
Ruling all the lands

I've Been Saved

I've been saved
I've told my friends
I've told my teacher
I was weak
But now I'm strong
I was poor
But now I'm rich
I was blind
But now I can see
I was out in the world
I was out in darkness
Then He brought me into the light
I thought battling with my hands was important
But He showed me to let Him fight my battle

By: Bryce Gill Flowers
Age: 7

Cast The First Stone

I said you were wrong
I pointed my finger at you
I tried to judge your heart
Knowing I'm guilty too

How can I do that
When both our frames are dust?
We both have faults and defects
We both were born out of lust

He who is without sin
Cast the first stone
And when you lift your head
All accusers should be gone

Forgive Me Lord

Lord please forgive me
I've been wrong today
The evil thoughts I have
Kept getting in my way

A better child is what
I would like to be
Please increase my faith
Draw me nearer to Thee

Have mercy on my soul
It's all in your power
Forgive me for my sins
I repent this very hour

Young People Stand

Young People in school
Head in the books
Ignore the pointed fingers
Ignore the strange looks

When the harasser comes
And starts to torture you
It only means your light
Is finally shining through

Shining through darkness
Shining through walls
Shining everywhere you go
Up and down the halls

Ignore the harasser
And pray in your heart
That one day from evil
He'll want to depart

Don't go for vengeance
It belongs to the Lord
Forgive in your heart
The Word is your sword

Talk to The Savior
Before your day starts
He'll be with you always
Alive in your heart

Name-calling, lies
And all of these things
Remember Young People
It was done to The King

The Blood

Did you hear about the blood
That's spotless and pure?
It went into every stream
It has the power to cure

Whatever the condition
Whatever the complaint
If you're dipped in the blood
Your soul won't have to faint

We must be baptized
Every soul must know
For the blood is in the water
Down in Jesus' Name, we must go

Our soul has been purchased
Jesus paid the price
Nothing else could do it
Nothing else could suffice

Thank you Lord for the blood
That went into the waters
Bringing back to you
Your lost sons and daughters

So don't it make you want to
Give God all the praise
Every minute, every hour
For the rest of your days?

The Gospel of The Kingdom
Is Being Preached

People say nothing is in Allendale
But that is not true
Jesus Christ is being preached
He's made my heart brand new

The Good News of Jesus
North, South, West and East
Every man's soul must taste of
This God Prepared Feast

On the menu four times per week
Is true bread from heaven
12:00 Noon on Sundays
Three nights half past seven

The Lord prepares a special meal
To nurture His children's soul
This bread cannot be purchased
It's free to the young and old

It's ringing up and down the street
It shall not return void
Some say they recognize the voice
Some say it's just some noise

It comes against our ways
It comes against our thoughts
It breaks down stubborn wills
It brings flesh to a naught

We need the words of life
Where ever we reside
I feel content in Allendale
With Jesus as my guide

The Kingdom of God is set up
In His children's hearts
When this old world shall end
The Kingdom of Heaven will start

Right on earth it will be
The Family of Jesus Christ
Still hearing the Everlasting Gospel
Still hearing the Words of Life

Lord I Thank You

Jesus:
My Knight In Shining Armour
Came and rescued me
I was imprisoned in my mind
I wanted so bad to be free

I labored day and night
But never received my pay
I couldn't help but work so hard
I knew no other way

I thought it was supposed to be
Crying, heartache and pain
I accepted death so easily
Sometimes I felt insane

I was driven by a force
That was not of Jesus Christ
A force of evil and darkness
My soul, Satan did heist

One day I heard about Jesus
And how He died for me
I wanted to meet This Jesus
Who died to set me free

I went to His House
And heard His spoken word
It went down in my heart
I became free, as the bird

He was speaking through a man
Saying "Repent and be baptized
You must go down in Jesus' name
For the new man to arise"

I looked around and realized
He was talking to my soul
He wanted to fill me with His Spirit
So that the mystery would unfold

I didn't know His way was simple
I didn't know it was so sweet
I thought I had to be good
To sit at Jesus' feet

He told me He had done it all
There was nothing I could do
Just believe He is the Son of God
Saving all colors, White and the Jew

I said, "Lord I thank you
For letting little me come
And serve The Man With All Power
Knowing I'm rotten and undone"

He didn't have to do it
But I'm so glad He did
My heavy load is gone
In Him, my life is hid

Give God The Glory

Glory to God
All praises too
Direct credit and honor
To whom it is due

For we can do nothing
On our own might
God controls it all
Even weight and height

Don't give me praises
Give them to The Son
His name is Jesus Christ
Surely, He is The One

Be Encouraged

Read this to someone
Who can't read or write
Tell them to be encouraged
Tell them it's all right

If they are naturally deaf
That's certainly okay
God will grant an inner ear
To hear what He has to say

Tell them if they can believe
When they hear God's Spoken Word
Be baptized in Jesus' Name
As proof that they have heard

For now the word is written
On the tables of our hearts
The Holy Ghost is in us
Never again to depart

My Testimony

One day I was unemployed
Craving a job so bad
I asked The Lord for one
He granted it, I was glad

I made a vow to Him
Because I love Him so
I said, "Nothing will separate us"
For there is no other help I know

He let me perform a task
That I had never done
I gave Him all the glory
For I deserved none

The job was going well
The most money I ever made
The Lord let me remember
That He is my shade

One day I was confronted
About the God that I serve
I was told that I was wrong
For giving Him honor He deserves

They said I was imposing
My faith on others
Being very disrespectful
To lost sisters and brothers

They wanted me to sign
A man made decree
I refused to do so
The Lord's too good to me

I said, "About my Father's Business,
That I Am,
He's the one, who let this happen,
Thank you Ma'am"!

I couldn't abandon my lover
He didn't abandon me
I was without a Savior
So He died on Calvary

As they sat in awe
They thought I had a plan
I said, "The Lord will provide"
To this day, in Him I stand

A Gangster's Cry

Guys in gangs
Looking for love
Bullying others
Displeasing The One above

Love is not love
If it's not of God
Who are you serving?
Don't you think it's odd?

To accept death from the Devil
When God offers life
Does the Devil care about you?
No! He kills you with the knife,

He kills you with drugs,
Hatred and guns
Jesus offers the opposite
Who will be that one?

To take a step down,
In order to move up?
In Jesus is success
In Him, nothing is corrupt

Now what you see
With your natural eyes
Is on its way down
Not on the rise

If you really knew
Where the enemy lay
You would love one another
Starting today

You are your greatest enemy:
Not your neighbor, fellowman,
Father or mother
Not your co-worker, 'X',
Sister or brother

Your enemy is a twin
Going everywhere you go
Your enemy is your outer man
Hating God–Didn't you know?

You have a soul
It needs to be saved
It's the real part of you
The part of you that craves

Craving to seek The Lord
While He may be found
Will you wait until too late?
Six feet under the ground?

Will you continue bullying others
And eventually die from hate?
Or love your brothers and sisters
And lay aside the extra weight?

You don't have to be bound
You don't have to play tough
Jesus paid the price for you
And what He paid, was certainly enough

Forever

Walk in His word
Speak in His word
Love in His word
He is The Way

Hope in His word
Trust in His word
Believe in His word
He is The Truth

Rejoice in His word
Stand in His word
Rest in His word
He is The Light

His Word
His Power
He Was
He ls

He Will Be
He Shall Be
Forever!

God Is

God is a spirit
Penetrating walls
Penetrating hate
His Power is All

God is a spirit
Loving women and men
No matter how evil
And sinful we've been

God is a spirit
Who once wrapped in flesh
To redeem our souls
Because we transgressed

God is a spirit
Not a color or feeling
We should magnify Him
Standing, sitting or kneeling

God Is Love!

Friend In Jesus

There's a friend that you need
A friend everyone should know
His name is Jesus Christ
He's been waiting on you since long ago

He won't send you away
He doesn't wish you ill
Instead His arms are spread
Saying, ''Whosoever Will''

He won't put you down
Like a brother sometimes do
Instead He'll pick you up
When it seems no one loves you

When you get in trouble
He won't turn His back
He'll stay and help you through
He's faithful and that's a fact

You can trust Him with your life
He has so much more to give
He'll exchange your life for His
And forever you will live

Grace Waited

Oh how patient is grace!

As my tongue killed daily
And my lips blessed not your name
spoke of only foolishness
Grace waited so patiently!

My eyes and heart beheld pride
My ears itched for ridicule
My heart sat blacker than night
Grace waited so patiently!

As my feet ran to mischief
As my confidence rested in man
As I breathed God given air
Grace waited so patiently!

Thank God For Grace!
From A Sinner Saved By Grace!

Stop It Mr. Bully

Tell me Mr. Bully
How does it make you feel
When you lock eyes with your victim
And see that he is real?

Do you realize he's your brother
And you're inflicting pain?
You're carefully carving scars
In his heart and his brain

Stop it Mr. Bully
You're breaking your brother's heart
Do you realize what you're doing
Throwing Satan's fiery darts

One day you'll face that pain
That you're putting your victim through
Then you'll stop and wonder why
This thing is happening to you

All of a sudden you'll remember
And say; "Now I know why,
I did this to my brother,
I thought I was getting by"

Remember Mr. Bully
Jesus sits high and looks low
He sees every thing you do
And knows everywhere you go

The Doctor Is In The City

The Doctor is in the city
He's the best one ever
He performed the first surgery
He exceeds the word clever

He doesn't use a knife
He won't put you to sleep
Don't worry about insurance
He loves to heal His sheep

If you have arthritis
Diabetes and heart trouble
If you are HIV Positive
If the life you live is double

He can fix it for you
If you can just believe
He took it all to the cross
And hung between two thieves

If your mind is unstable
And it wanders here and there
He'll take it and give you His
That's just how much He cares

The Doctor is in the city
Preaching Jesus to the poor
Ready to teach you His ways
Ways you never knew before

Do you want to be made whole?
Or do you want to die?
Will you accept the gift of life?
For The Doctor is nigh

The Hidden Man of the Heart

Down in the heart
Is a precious throne
On it sits a King
Your mansion is His home

For our weary souls
He came to give us rest
Sin tired us out
So He gave us His best

The Holy Ghost dwells
In the hearts of men
Controlling our every move
Telling us how and when

We don't have to worry
We don't have to cry
The Comforter is here
Sent from On High

Today At Work

Today I thank you Lord
For how you touched your sheep
It wasn't the alarm clock
That awoke me from my sleep

Someone's clock kept ringing
As the spirit departed the flesh
Another switched the clock off
For you required eternal rest

Lord let me start this day
Cherishing each breath I take
Taking all mistakes for love
Learning from the errors I make

Today what I desire
Is to fulfill some intentions
But without your present help
I can do nothing that I mention

If my boss roughs me up
Please let him understand
You're the only one who's right
That's why we're in your hands

When I'm about to argue
Lord, please seal my lips
When the pressure is turned up high
Please Lord, don't let me flip

Please don't let me complain
For what seems bad is good
Let me count my blessings
And be grateful, as I should

If you require of my soul
Before I return home
Please receive my spirit
So the spirit doesn't roam

Out Came The Son

The night was so dark
But Son Light was near
I couldn't give up
There was no time to fear

Son Light appeared
The clouds rolled away
It dried up my tears
It brightened my day

High Tower

Men are victims
Of harassment too
What would you do Mr.
If it were you?

Would you take it upon
Yourself to solve?
Would you call the police
And get them involved?

Would you broadcast it
And let it be known?
Would you keep the harasser's
Cover from being blown?

Well there is A Man
He has All Power
He's highly recommended
For He's The High Tower

Not a thought is thought
Without His knowledge
Real wisdom comes from Him
Not from a college

Your harasser can't outsmart Him
Neither outrun
Once He takes your case
The battle is won

Put your confidence in Jesus
He won't let you down
Whenever you need Him
He's always around

Maybe your harasser
Will try Him too
Jes us is available
He loves them and you

Spiritual Picnic

Have you ever been to a picnic
With many tasty dishes
The variety was very great
Everything looked so delicious?

You began to make your choice
Not wanting to seem so greedy
You asked for just a little
Not wanting to appear so needy?

Well, I went to a picnic
Where the food was mighty great
An evening of spiritual food
Was spread on my plate

After I ate the natural
The Lord began to speak
My heart started lusting
For the Word is what it seeks

I was fed bread from heaven
I could get it no other way
Than spoken through God's Mouth
I ate what He had to say

I tell you, It tasted so good
1 didn't want to move
I ate all that He offered
Not caring who disapproved

For this food straight from Jesus
Was strictly for my soul
The highlight of the picnic
The food that made me whole

When I Am Gone

When my time is up on earth
Please don't cry for me
For my Father knows what's best
He's the one who has set me free

I didn't come here to stay
You knew this day would come
This old flesh must go back
To dust where it is from

My spirit has separated
From the natural man
Praise God, I'm so glad!
For my spirit, God has a plan!

How can we have life eternal
If the body never sheds?
The soul must depart from the body
It's alive and not dead

So if you visit my grave
Remember, I'm not there
The real me is resting
In my Savior, The One who cares

A Wandering Spirit

A spirit is headed your way
It is not of The Lord
Coming to torment you
And pierce you like a sword

It's looking for a house
A place to call home
Once it dwells in your heart
You'll begin to roam

The spirit of harassment
A spirit that's not free
Came to bind, came to kill
Came to steal you away from Thee

It'll send you on a mission
It has work to be done
Killing brothers and sisters
Fooling you it's of The Son

When the spirit is finished
Your body will fall down
The spirit leaps and laughs
As your body is lowered into the ground

Then it finds someone new
To do its evil deeds
Their body then gets used
Planting damnable seeds

So pray that the evil spirit
Does not ask God for you
It gets permission from Jesus
He controls what spirits do

Your Presence Lord

Grace me with your presence
Lord, I love you so
With your blessed presence
Anywhere, my soul can go

There is no real joy
Not a place on earth
If you're not there
Existence has no worth

Grace me with your presence
Hide me in your word
I want to be where you are
It's you my soul prefers

There Are No Bastard Children

Children, you have a Father
A bastard is no such
He gave His life for you
He loves you so much

You are no less than others
Calling on His sweet name
You have a right to praise Him
You have a right just the same

What the dictionary says
To you it doesn't apply
We're the children of God Almighty
The Strong Tower On High

Bullies Hate Bullying

If it wasn't for the bully
I never would have known
How empty is my sister
She feels so all-alone

Because of that great void
She's feeling in her life
She lashes out at others
Like an unloved wife

I don't like seeing my sister
So full of hate and grief
must tell her about Jesus
He's her only true relief

I must tell about His goodness
And His merciful way
Because of this One Man
We can look up and live today

She must go through the door
Somebody has the keys
It's the Men of God Preaching Jesus
If she can just believe

Bullies hate bullying
They only need direction
Not negative but positive
They need love not rejection

Unloved Touch

Someone touched me today
It was one out of nine
It wasn't like the others
It wasn't genuine

I didn't like the statement
That the touch made
My heart began to speak
As the words of life played

The touch came from someone
Who thinks his wants are a must
Searching for something more
And is guided by its lusts

Can the touch become subject
If it hears God's Word preached?
Only God can prick a heart
There's not a soul He can't reach

Teach Me Jesus

Teach me Lord
What to say
In all situations
On any day

You're wisdom's author
And also knowledge
You're smartest of smarts
Including doctors of college

If I say what I think
If I speak that I know
It carries no weight
It amounts to zero

So teach me Lord
What to say
In all situations
On any day

Standing At The Crossroad

Standing at the crossroad
Which road should I take
Lord please tell me
The choice that I should make

I want to do what's pleasing
In Thine eyesight
If you don't direct me Lord
I won't do what is right

My way is dark without you
I simply cannot see
Standing at the crossroad
Waiting for you is me

Surrender

We all have a weakness
Whatever it may be
Jesus still loves us
His love is a guarantee

We all are sinners
We all fall short
We all need Jesus
He is our fort

Sin is not divided
As large or small
Sin is not divided
As short or tall

Sin is not divided
As rich or poor
All sin spells SIN
We've all sinned before

Our sins are in remission
Jesus took out the sting
He arose with all power
Praise God for our King

So surrender to Jesus
Bring your habits too
He'll let you die daily
And bring out the real you

Remember Me Lord

In the Kingdom
I want to reign
With my Jesus
Where life is gain

Lord will you please
Remember thou me
Let the Kingdom
Be my destiny!

Soul Food

All that you can touch and feel
Is here but for a season
To lose your soul over earthly things
Would be a foolish reason

Concentrate on the soul
The part we cannot see
The most valuable part about us
The only part that's free

What the soul must have
Is not this earthly bread
But every word from God's Mouth
Is how the soul is fed

My Soul Is Free

Today you called my name
However, I did not hear
I'm absent from the body
Dry up your many tears

I stayed with you a season
And now that time is up
Flesh can't live forever
Because it is corrupt

Sin dwells in the flesh
That's why it has to die
Aren't you glad I'm free?
It's the will of the One On High

My soul is satisfied
And happy as can be
Singing, "Glory Hallelujah,
The inner man is free"!

Life has just begun
It's time for real joy
My heart has never known
The greatness God employs

I'm absent from the body
I'm present with Thee
Freedom is now complete
Jesus made a way for me

Inside of A Harasser

Harassers hate for
The grass to be green
Harassers hate for
Life's beauty to be seen

Harassers love
Poking fun at you
Because of the fact
That they are sad and blue

Harassers are upset
They want to be heard
So they choose the form
Of a mockingbird

A harasser could be you
Could be me
Lord help us please
Not to be

Harassers can't see the light
At the end of the tunnel
So they accept darkness
And live in a funnel

They're tossed about
Where ever the winds blow
Because they never stand still
Long enough to grow

Just call on His name
He died for us all
Admit your game
Short, thick, skinny and tall

He took our sins
To the cross
We have no reason
To be lost

Jesus Is Worthy

At the break of dawn
Jesus is worthy!

In the heat of the day
Jesus is worthy!

In the darkest hour
Jesus is worthy!

Right now, this moment,
Jesus is worthy to be praised!

Hold Up Your Light

Hold up your light!
Hold up your light!
Hold it up for Jesus!

If the Holy Ghost lives in you
God's given you His best
You've got to go through trials
You've got to go through tests

Don't be ashamed of Jesus
Just hold up your light
He'll take you to deeper depths
He'll take you to higher heights

Hold up your light
Hold up your light
Hold it up for Jesus!

If The Son Didn't Shine

If The Son didn't shine
The flowers wouldn't grow
If The Son didn't shine
Love couldn't show

If The Son didn't shine
Darkness would prevail
If The Son didn't shine
All success would fail

What is a day
Without The Son?
Let The Son shine
And Thy Will be done

Forgive, Forget

Long before you were born
Long before you knew
Lies were told on The Savior
What do you think about you?

Don't hate your lying brother
For the lie he has told
God is The Truth, every man a liar
All races, young and old

Embrace your lying brother
When the lie is told on you
Provoke him to love my child
Jesus died for him too

Forgive and forget things done
Forgive and forget things said
Shouldn't you forgive your brother?
Or hold a grudge instead?

When the thoughts come to mind
Of what's been done to you
Ask The Lord for the power
To push those thoughts on through

Keep pushing those old thoughts
Keep pushing them away
Soon you'll have new thoughts
It'll be a brand new day

All About Jesus

When Jesus wants to use you
Will you pack up and run?
Hoping He'll find another
To display the works of The Son?

Will you give the Devil credit
And say he's testing you?
Will you give in to pressure
And pretend you never knew?

That in Christ we have afflictions
And very light trials
As part of our cross
As part of self denial

If He chooses your vessel
To show His works through
Count it as a joy
He saw fit to use you

For the flesh is no good
The spirit quickens our soul
It's all about Jesus
The Good News must be told

It's all about Jesus
His works must be shown
It's all about Jesus
His power must be known

It's all about Jesus
Salvation is free
It's all about Jesus
Not you, not me

Bright Light

There's A Light shining so bright
All other light is dim
There's A Light shining so great
Sparkling like a precious gem

There's A Light shining so far
It reaches into the dark
There's A Light shining forever
It has no beginning mark

A Sinner's Friend

Forever I will need you Lord
In me please abide
Forever I will need you Lord
In Thee, I must hide

Jesus Christ
Is a sinner's friend
He called me out
He took me in

He died in my stead!

Are you standing
His Word is true
If you stand
He'll deliver you

Look at Jesus dying
For our sins
Died for the sins
Of wicked men

Jesus Christ
Is a sinner's friend
He called me out
He took me in

He died in my stead!

Saved By Grace

I was a lost sinner
Lost, I used to be
Now I'm a saved sinner
But still a sinner–that's me!

Thank God for Jesus
I'm saved by His grace
He extended my time
So I could seek His Face

He was never lost
I was the one
But He found me
Thank God for His Son!

Stop Looking and See

See The Beloved
See His grace
See His long suffering
See His sweet ways

See how He loves
See how He forgives
See how He cares
And wants us to live

See past my faults
See past my sins
See past my flesh
Something greater is within

You're passing Jesus
Every single day
See within your brother
Stop looking the other way!

Magnify Jesus Christ

Magnify Jesus Christ
He's so much greater
Than our faults and defects
Exalt Him now, not later

An exclamation mark
Goes after His Name
For He took away our guilt
And all sin and shame

His Name is good
For good is He
He's the perfect God
For all men to see

Magnify The Lord
Great, Great God
Surely He is worthy
His way is not odd!

A Mother's Love

A mother loves her children
Her love is so deep
But there's One who watches over them
Even when they are asleep

The children belong to Jesus
They aren't hers to keep
He was crucified for them
They're His lost sheep

So to prove a mother's love
Have your children baptized
In the name of Jesus
Where soul salvation lies

Only water can remove
The inherited sin
Committed by Adam
And passed down to men

Then came a man
Named Jesus Christ
He took the sting out of death
So that we can have life

Let the children learn His ways
And not the ways of man
If you truly love your children
For Jesus you'll urge them to stand

A Bully Needs

A bully needs peace
On the inward part
A bully needs love
Down in their heart

A bully needs joy
To come into their life
Joy overrides misery
Joy overrides strife

A bully needs hope
That a change will come
A bully needs Jesus'
Will to be done

How does a bully
Even know how to change?
When his heart is dark
And his god is strange?

Start by calling
On Jesus' name
His love is unconditional
His word will tame

Jesus specializes
In the impossible
If you can
Believe the invisible

I dare you to call
On the All in All
He can stop the bullying
Before the bully falls

False Accusers

Did you hear the nasty rumor
That's spreading around town
The more it is repeated
The faster it gets around

Smile when you see thine accusers
And they will wonder why
Such a smile is on your face
When you're supposed to cry

If thine accuser has witnesses
And they too seek to kill
Your witness is on the inward part
Just be quiet, just be still

I'm Rich

I may not have thousands
Millions or more
I may not have land
Cars and clothes galore

I'm so happy
That I know one thing
My Father is rich
My Father's The King

He owns it all
He has All Power
He's the life giver
From humans to flowers

In His Word
My blessings lie
For in His Word
You live and don't die

I'm rich in His Spirit
That's enough for me
In Jesus Christ
My soul wants to be

Keep Me Lord

Lord keep my soul
You know how it's done
Keep it while with patience
This Christian Race I run

Lord keep my mind
Don't let it waver
Don't let it wander
Please do me this favor

Lord keep my heart
Let it lust after you
Don't let it stop
Before this life is through

Lord please keep me!

Jesus Is Mine

Jesus is mine
I am His
Does this sound simple?
Because it is

He loves me
That's why He died
I love Him
In Him I abide

Me and Jesus
Jesus and me
Together forever
Unto eternity

Pray For Your Enemies

If you're a bully's victim
And your head is down
Lift it up this instant
Smile–remove the frown

For the bully's behavior
Is no reflection on you
He shows what's in his heart
He shows his point of view

When you're not his victim
He'll choose another
He's so unhappy
He torments his brother

When you pray for yourself
Pray for the bully the same
His soul is in great trouble
But help lies in one name

That name is Jesus Christ!

Female Harassment

When girls exclude a friend
And refuse to talk to her
Harassment is taking place
Now why does this occur?

A spirit has been accepted
That is not of The Lord
The friendship has divided
For a lack of God's Word

Get it together girls
Don't let the Devil win
For the Devil loves division
Are you going to let him in?

What has he done for you?
Except cause you grief and pain
He had you on death row
Until Jesus died and rose again

Will you harass your friend?
Or show forth true love?
Will you represent Satan?
Or will it be the one above?

Words With Meaning

Someone said I've always
Been good at using words
But what good is that
If the words are never heard

Someone taught me new words
That I have never known
Straight from The Bishop's Mouth
God's seed has been sown

These new words that I know
Are not like all the others
For these words have life
Sent to me from my Lover

These words are Jesus Christ
The Word is what He is
They live down in my heart
He gave me what is His

We're Free

The verdict has been given
Our soul is free
Give God the Glory
We have the victory

The law has been abolished
Salvation has appeared
Jesus Christ bought it
Evening time is here

The spirit now quickens
No more laws of the flesh
We're free to do God's Will
Lord let my soul say yes!

The Rock

At the top of the highest mountain
Sits a Solid Rock so true
The Rock is irreplaceable
It's there for me and you

The Rock will let you come
And live inside
And you will be protected
For The Rock will be your guide

When the storm arises
And needs must be fulfilled
Continue to trust in The Rock
The Rock works when we're still

You won't have to fall
When you reside in The Rock
Danger seeks to destroy you
But The Rock will block

The Rock will live in you
That's if you so desire
If you let it be so
Your soul will never tire

Spirit of Harassment

Harassment at the school
Harassment on the job
Harassment in manners
That will make you feel robbed

Harassment in the mail
Harassment on the phone
Harassment in odd places
Even on your way home

Don't be discouraged
Jesus is alive
He knows your harasser
He knows their drive

He knows their spirit
Which is not of Him
For He ordained it
Its power is dim

His power is light
The greatest of all
He'll fight your battles
So that you won't fall

For He is able
To keep you from falling
On His name
We should all be calling

Leave the harasser
In His hands
And in Him
Take your stand

He knows exactly
What to do
He was harassed
He made it through

His hands are firm
They are strong
He's always right
And never wrong

He'll handle your harasser
In ways you wouldn't
He'll handle your harasser
In ways you couldn't

Good, Bad, No Credit

If your credit is good
If your credit is bad
If you have no credit
You shouldn't feel sad

What does credit have to do
With soul salvation?
Salvation is of the Lord
And we're His creation

All that we owed
Was nailed to the cross
Our debts have been paid
By Jesus Christ–The Boss

What ever you need is in Jesus
Your needs He will supply
Just seek after His righteousness
To you–He'll draweth nigh

He has promised us clothes
He has promised us food
He won't renege on His promises
Like us when in our moods

He knows what we must have
So much better than us
He's able to determine
Our needs from our lusts

Repent

A Lawyer is recommended
Who's never lost a case
He represents each gender
He represents each race

A Lawyer is recommended
Who knows what we need
When This Lawyer speaks
Everyone must take heed

A Lawyer is recommended
Who knows the defendant well
We can be truthful with Him
To Him, your secrets tell

He looks into our hearts
And sees what is there
He understands our mistakes
He's forgiving and so fair

Let Him represent you
He doesn't charge a cent
He wants to defend you
He wants you to repent

Female Bully

You're a bully
You're a female
You're losing ground
You're about to fail

Bullying makes you feel good
Makes you feel in control
Makes you feel empowered
Like you can't be told

It makes you feel you know the way
That you're supposed to go
Your mind has played a trick on you
For surely you don't know

If you want to be successful
You will have to be told
For our way is not The Lord's
His way is true and bold

Ask for an humble heart
Ask Him to teach you His ways
Ask Him for an ear to hear
In this last and evil day

And then you'll know all power
Belongs to Jesus Christ
Thc One who gives us strength
The One who gave us life

Royal Priesthood

I belong to a Royal Priesthood
Because of nothing to do with me
But because of King Jesus
Who died on Calvary

He carried a heavy cross
Was beaten all night long
Just to prove He loved me
In spite of all of my wrong

I've been washed in His blood
The inherited sin is gone
I've been born into His family
At last I feel at home

His people are peculiar
We've been set apart
Pre-destined for the Kingdom
He knew me from the start

I'm the one who sinned
I'm the one to blame
But all because He loves me so
He died, He arose, The King came

Seek The Lord

What would you take
In exchange for your soul?
Would it be sterling silver?
Would it be pure gold?

What would be sufficient
To swap for your soul?
Do you believe things
Can make you feel whole?

You can have things
Don't let them have you
Falling in love with things
Is what we sometimes do

When things reign in the heart
Then it becomes sin
God is a jealous God
Being mindful of men

One throne can't have two kings
No! It just can't be!
Love one and hate the other
The one you hate will flee

Seek ye first God's Kingdom
And all of His righteousness
He'll give you what you need
Your soul, He wants to bless

Lover of Lovers

There's a name that's worthy
To be lifted up
If you lift this name
He'll fill your cup

Jesus Christ is the name
How awesome is He
My King of Kings
Mighty Prince of Peace

What a blessed name
In your heart to receive
He's the Lover of Lovers
No more will you grieve

Itching Ears

When the gossiping starts
We can disappear
Don't get caught up in it
Don't lend a listening ear

Speak on the victim's behalf
If you don't walk away
Silence gives consent
Saying, "It is okay"

Don't believe in hearsay
How can we know?
The carrier could be lying
So watch the seeds we sow

So easily we become a judge
Which is not our place
Pointing fingers here and there
Behind the back and not to the face

What's in a person's heart
We definitely can't say
Jesus is the Heart Man
Dwelling in hearts today

Next time our index finger
Points in the outward direction
Turn it toward ourselves
And see if we see perfection

Love

Love covers faults
Love covers defects
Love dwells in places
That only God can connect

Love takes hate
And tosses it away
Love keeps loving
No matter what people say

Love is of God
It went to the cross
Love suffered pain
So our souls wouldn't be lost

Love laid in a tomb
Three days and three nights
Love arose with all power
And gave us a right

To Eternal Joy!

In The Evening

In the evening
It's time to go home
Leisure time is over
No more time to roam

Parents want children
Inside by night
Because home is safe
And everything is all right

Morning has come
And now it has passed
Noonday has come
It wasn't the last

Evening is here
End your venture
This call is the last
You can rest assure

All lost sheep
Must come home
The Master is calling
Soon, evening will be gone

Order Form

To order additional copies, fill out this form and send it along with your check or money order to: Hermeione Flowers, 210 Dunbar St., Allendale, SC 29810

Cost per copy $11.95 plus $2.00 P&H.

Ship _____ copies of *The Son Did Rise (A Book of Spiritual Poems)* to:

Name_____

Address: _____

City/State/Zip: _____

❑ Check box for signed copy

Please tell us how you found out about this book.

☐ Friend	☐ Internet
☐ Book Store	☐ Radio
☐ Newspaper	☐ Magazine
☐ Other _____	

www.ingramcontent.com/pod-product-compliance
Lightning Source LLC
Chambersburg PA
CBHW061456040426
42450CB00008B/1386